Introduction to
BATIK

D1254662

Introduction to
BATIK

Heather Griffin & Margaret Hone

NORTH LIGHT BOOKS

Cincinnati, Ohio

WITHDRAWN

028050

Introduction to batik

Batik is a very ancient craft dating back at least two thousand years. It can be defined as a method of applying a coloured design on to textiles by waxing those parts that are not to be dyed. Evidence of its practice has been discovered in most Eastern and Middle Eastern countries including India, China, Japan, Persia and Egypt, but although its actual source is unknown, it was on the island of Java in Indonesia that the art reached its peak of development. Through the centuries Javanese craftsmen have perfected the art, reflecting the culture and religion of their country in the richness of colours and the detail of the designs on their fabrics. These traditional designs have been passed on from one generation to another and are mainly based on the flora and fauna of their surroundings and this form of expression adapts to society now as easily as it did so many years ago.

Batik has evolved around the principle that wax and water repel each other, therefore an area of fabric that has been covered with wax is unable to accept dye. The Indonesian word 'tik', meaning a drop (referring to the small drops of hot wax), shows how the word 'batik' was derived. It is an exciting medium for beginners to explore because there is always an element of surprise when the wax is removed from the fabric and the hidden effect is revealed. Careful waxing should ensure that the surprise is a pleasant one and not the reverse! The effect one colour has on another is particularly exciting, even to the more experienced batik artist. With adequate supervision, children enjoy experimenting with batik. They talk to us at craft fairs about their work and show a great deal of interest in our designs.

White pure cotton, (or white pure silk), is the best material to use for batik. Hot wax is applied to the fabric in the areas that are to be kept white and then the dye is added. The lightest colour is the first dye. The fabric is then waxed in those areas that are to be kept in this first colour and the process repeated with a second colour. Waxing and dyeing in this way is continued until the desired effect is achieved; the last and darkest colour being black. Since colours are merging during the dyeing process, in unwaxed areas, it is important to adhere to a particular colour scale. For example, if the first dye is red and the second blue, keep in mind that the result is not blue but violet. Once all the dyeing is complete, the wax is then removed revealing the design.

Fine cracks can occur in the wax during the process, or can be deliberately planned as part of the design. When the wax cracks, the dye penetrates the fabric in these places and gives the batik its distinctive veined look, though some artists prefer to have little or no cracking at all.

Every batik is a one-off original. You may, of course, attempt to reproduce a previously successful design, but it will always have an originality of its own because of the nature of the craft. It is impossible to duplicate exactly the application, or the random crackle pattern of the wax, or even guarantee the precise colour values. Your personal approach to this exciting medium will ensure that you develop your own particular style and understanding of the potential of batik.

The Hollyford Track by Heather Griffin
Wax and several different coloured dyes are applied to white cotton, before the waxed fabric is cracked and dipped in dark green dye, giving the effect of trees and foliage. Further waxing and dyeing creates the darker tree trunks and shadows. For detailed instructions on how to make the picture opposite, see pages 46 and 47.

Uses for batik fabrics

In any area of design where a fabric is the main constituent, batik can play an exciting part in the decoration. We have shown a variety of designs on the following pages, including coats, blouses, tops, bows, scarves, a wall hanging and picture; there are many more applications for this craft and a few are listed below.

Clothes: there is a great deal of satisfaction to be gained by wearing clothes made from your own original batik design. The simplest clothes can easily be made by you if you wish, but it is also possible to buy ready made white cotton and silk garments and set about creating your own batik design on them. Children's clothes look particularly attractive.

If you want to make your own clothes, there are several ways of applying a batik design.

1. Retain the material in one piece with the shapes of the pattern pieces lightly drawn on, thus enabling you to see where your batik design will be on the finished garment.
2. Having several smaller pieces of material (not cut to pattern).
3. Having material cut to pattern but on a slightly larger scale than the finished pattern pieces, to allow for a certain amount of fraying at the edges, or slight shrinkage. The batik pieces are then finally cut to the correct size.

Scarves: this is a very attractive method of using batik, especially in silk. Scarves can also be bought ready made in white silk or you can, of course, make your own in either silk or cotton (see opposite and page 28).

Belts and hair bows: these simple items make original personal or bazaar gifts, (see pages 26 and 27 for bows).

Wallhangings: these can be quite basic, with very few colours, through to complicated pictures requiring much creative planning.

Soft furnishings: batik may be used for many household purposes such as blinds, curtains, cushion covers, lampshades, tablecloths, bedspreads, all designed to complement your own colour schemes.

Mirror and picture frames: this is a most original way of adding a personal touch to ordinary household items.

Greetings cards: if you are reluctant to tackle a large area of fabric, begin by experimenting with a small remnant which can be mounted as a personal greetings card.

Soft toys: these can allow you to give full rein to your imagination. Tigers and tabby cats lend themselves particularly well to this application of the craft.

Perhaps you can think of other applications for a textile which features your own unique design.

Silk scarf designs by Margaret Hone
A luxurious, beautifully coloured silk scarf is the perfect gift or accessory. Simple designs can be applied to bought scarves, or hand-made scarves can be created from odd pieces of silk, and one or two dyes applied.
The central blue and white scarf is coloured with just one dye. It is worked flat on a sheet of greaseproof paper and an abstract design drawn straight on to the fabric with wax, leaving larger areas free to take the dye. It is then dipped in blue dye and when dry the wax is removed (see page 19 for instructions on removing wax from silk).
When using two or more dyes, follow the method shown on pages 21–25. More detailed instructions for applying batik to scarves are found on page 28.

Design sources

Ideas for batik designs are everywhere. If you are already an accomplished artist you will probably have your own sources of ideas and sketches to work from, but a beginner in batik can just as easily find inspiration.

Before beginning, you must decide what you are going to make and then consider the most suitable type of design. This could be abstract, representational or geometric. Always bear in mind the measurements of your material against the scale of your design.

It is not necessary to be a superb artist to create a good design. A simple composition, just based on random blocks of colour, can be very successful. Inspiration for design can be drawn from many sources; nature, photographs, postcards, text books, paintings, magazines, posters, greetings cards and everyday objects.

Nature is a never ending source of inspiration. So are household pets and the plants, flowers and trees in your garden. Fruits and vegetables, when cut open, give unusual abstract designs, as do patterns made by clouds, waves and rock formations. A camera is invaluable for instantly recording something that catches your eye, or you can make sketches with detailed colour notes.

As colour is such an essential part of batik, it is a most important feature of the design and must be carefully planned in advance.

Sailboard and landscape designs by Heather Griffin
The two contrasting pictures on this page show details taken from batik shirts. They illustrate effectively how ideas for design can be found almost anywhere. For detailed instructions in how to create these designs, see pages 39–41.

Equipment and materials

Before you can begin any batik project, make sure that you have all the necessary equipment and materials available. They are as follows:
Fabric
Wooden frames
Drawing pins, safety pins, dressmaking pins or masking tape
Soft pencil, for drawing or tracing the design on to the fabric
Wax
Wax pot or a double saucepan
Brushes
Tjantings
Dye bath
Cold water dyes and fixing agents as recommended by the manufacturers
Large saucepan or metal bucket
Plastic buckets
Wooden tongs
Cleaning solvent
Rubber gloves
Plastic apron
Plastic clothes pegs
Teaspoons
Jam jars
Newspapers, greaseproof paper
Tracing paper
Paper tissues or kitchen roll

Fabrics

These must be manufactured from natural fibres, such as pure cotton, linen, muslin, poplin, silk and satin. It is best to wash all fabrics before beginning to work on them, to remove any dressing that may effect the penetration of the dyes. Cotton can be boiled if necessary. Synthetic fabrics are not suitable as they do not hold the dye satisfactorily.

Wooden frames

The fabric has to be stretched over a wooden frame before applying the hot wax. Ready made, adjustable batik frames can be purchased from craft shops. These are excellent, but expensive. Alternatively oil painting stretcher frames can be used. These come in a variety of sizes and the soft wood facilitates the use of drawing pins. Old picture frames can also be used, but they are often made from harder wood. You can, of course, make up your own simple wooden frame.

adjustable batik frame

notches at intervals to allow for adjustment to different sizes of fabric

It is a good idea to have one frame bound with strips of old sheeting and plastic, to be kept for use with silk and fine fabrics so the material can be attached to the frame with dressmakers' pins. If the silk is very fine it can be attached to the frame with masking tape or alternatively you could work without a frame. The silk should be laid out on a flat surface over a sheet of greaseproof paper before applying the wax.

frame

frame bound with strips of fabric

Wax

Wax is sold in a variety of forms – fine grains, flakes, discs or blocks. Find the one that suits you best. Experiment on small pieces of fabric, before attempting a larger batik.

Paraffin wax is probably the easiest to use. This can be used on its own, giving a greater cracking effect if desired. Beeswax used on its own gives virtually no cracking at all. Microcrystalline wax is less expensive to buy and gives a similar effect to beeswax. Batik wax is a mixture of beeswax and paraffin wax and is especially made for batik. It is available in most craft shops.

Wax pot

A wax pot is a special piece of equipment which is used specifically for heating and melting wax. It is thermostatically controlled and is the most efficient method of heating the wax. The design of the pot is such that the risk of hot wax spilling is minimal. Wax pots are available from most craft suppliers. Take care not to let the hot wax level drop below the 'minimum' mark.

wax pot

reservoir for wax

temperature control knob

If you do not wish to go to this expense, the wax can also be heated in a double saucepan, which is kept solely for this purpose. Zinc pots should *not* be used for melting wax, but enamel pots are fine. If you are using a double saucepan, care must be taken to:
a) not let the water boil away
b) not let the wax drop on to the hot cooker, as it can ignite.

The wax should be gently heated until it flows like water, and will impregnate the fabric fibres.

If spilt wax should ignite always smother the flames – never pour water on to the wax.

Brushes

Several brushes are necessary and these are used either for applying wax, or for painting dye on to the fabric.

It is advisable to use cheap oil brushes for waxing, or household paint brushes are useful. They are available in a variety of sizes ranging from 6 mm – 10 cm (⅛ – 4 in). A very small pointed brush can be used for fine lines.

Brushes with stiff bristles are best because the wax can be pushed directly into the cloth. Natural hair bristles last longer and do not become damaged as quickly as synthetic ones, but they are more expensive. A brush should never be used for anything else once wax gets into its bristles.

You will also need brushes of various sizes which must be kept exclusively for painting dye on to the batik.

Tjantings

These are traditional batik tools and they are used for drawing lines of wax on to the fabric, or sometimes for filling in larger areas where care is needed. They can be bought from most craft suppliers and are available in different sizes to produce thick or thin lines; they have one, two or three spouts.

A small amount of hot wax is held in a metal reservoir; this flows sparingly from the small spout or spouts, making fine lines for precise work.

Dye bath

Any suitable large container can be used and this could be a purpose-made dye bath or a plastic gravel tray purchased from your local ironmonger or garden centre. These trays come in a variety of sizes. The dye bath should be large enough to allow the batik to be kept flat when submerged and with enough room for it to be moved about; it should also be cleaned thoroughly after use.

Cold water dyes

Cold water dyes are readily available in powder form and in a large range of colours. They are mixed with fixatives according to the manufacturers' instructions. When using dyes avoid skin contact by using rubber gloves and take care not to inhale the dye powder. As many dyes are poisonous, keep them well away from food at all times.

Saucepan or metal bucket

Use a large saucepan or metal bucket for boiling the wax out of your cotton batik material. Never boil silk (see page 19 for instructions on removing wax from silk).

Extras

Tracing paper can be used to transfer a design on to your chosen fabric.

Plastic buckets are useful for containing cold water during the wax removal process.

Wooden tongs are necessary for handling the hot material.

Cleaning solvent is required for removing minute traces of wax from the fabric.

Rubber gloves and a plastic apron are most important for the protection of your hands and clothes.

Clothes pegs must be plastic so the dye does not penetrate the peg, as this colour may be transferred during the repeat dyeing process. Also plastic pegs are easier to wash and keep clean.

Teaspoons and jam jars are useful for mixing and storing dyes.

Newspaper can be laid flat as a working surface when dyeing and it is also invaluable as protection during the waxing and dyeing processes.

Greaseproof paper can be used as a waxing surface and it is also useful for keeping apart double thicknesses of fabric, if front and back designs are different.

Absorbent paper is used in the 'ironing-off' of wax process and is handy for mopping up any surplus dye.

three examples of tjantings

Colour planning

The most simple batik can be produced by waxing white material and dipping it in one colour, with the wax deliberately cracked to give the traditional veined batik look. Lovely cotton clothes can be made from a basic colour scheme like this. We have illustrated this method with simple bows (see pages 26 and 27) and babies T-shirts (see page 15). Fabrics should always be washed before use, to remove any oils and dressings.

It is easier at first to use closely related colours when planning a slightly more complicated batik, as some areas of colour will overlap. As each colour is added to the batik it will affect the previous colour. Pre-planning the colours for your work is most important. Time spent in writing down the progression of colours to be used is well worthwhile and could save a lot of problems later on.

The different coloured dyes can be mixed together either in the powder or made-up liquid form. They can also be overlapped on the fabric, to give you many more exciting colours. You can also increase the range of colours greatly by mixing them together.

The primary colours are red, yellow and blue, and these can be mixed together to give secondary colours; yellow and blue mixed together give green; red and yellow give orange; red and blue give purple, (see colour wheel opposite).

To be quite sure of your colours when using dyes, it is best to buy some secondary colours such as turquoise, brown and olive green, rather than relying on achieving the right mix; or be prepared to experiment! Be careful to mix a sufficient quantity of dye for the area to be covered, as it is very difficult to get an exact match if you should run out and have to mix more dye.

The proportion of the various dye affects the final colour. For example, a light red and a strong blue will give a different hue from a strong red and a very pale blue. The dye will dry to a lighter colour than it appears when wet and will also become lighter again when the cloth has been finally boiled out. Learning to gauge this is something that only experience will teach you.

The type of material used can also affect the intensity of the colour, so it is a good idea to test the dyes on small samples of your material before proceeding. When the dye has dried on your samples you will be able to judge whether the colours are correct.

In planning your design remember that the lightest colour should always be dyed first and the rest gradated according to shade, as dark colours cannot be made lighter. Remember too that every successive colour influences the previous one. Therefore, in more complicated colour schemes it is necessary to 'wax out' not only the light colours but also the areas that you wish to remain unaffected by the next dye. For example, in a colour scheme of blue, white and yellow, wax the white area *and* the area that will be dyed blue, then dye yellow. After the dye has dried, boil the wax out, then re-wax the area that is to be kept white *and* the area to be kept yellow and dye blue.

Any area of colour can be added by painting a dye on to either the plain white material or an area that has previously been dyed (see page 18). This is mainly useful for small areas that are enclosed by wax. A gradated wash (useful for large areas such as skies) can be achieved by tilting the stretched batik and painting the dye from the top, weakening with water as you progress downwards. You can, of course, combine any of the above methods when dyeing your fabric.

Mixing primary colours
red + yellow = orange
red + blue = purple
blue + yellow = green

13

How to begin

Decide on the item you are going to make. There are many ideas contained in this book or you can make up your own project. Choose your design and then follow this procedure.

Preparing the fabric

If you are a beginner, it is advisable to use cotton. However, once you have become used to this fabric, you can progress on to other materials.

Projects on silk can be very exciting. Take care to choose a suitable weight of silk for your purpose. We have used medium weight silk for the garments in this book – crepe de Chine, satin, and silk twill. Lightweight silk can be used for scarves and pictures. The method of working on silk is basically the same as that for cotton, with some additional points to remember, which are covered below and in the following sections.

Before cutting your fabric, wash it by hand to remove any dressing. *Never under any circumstances boil silk*! When cutting, allow enough overlap all the way round for pinning the fabric to the frame. About 5-7 cms (2-3 ins) should be enough. We find it is better to attach light-weight silk to a frame with masking tape, because dressmakers' pins could damage the fabric. Alternatively you could lay the silk on a flat surface over a sheet of greaseproof paper, before applying the wax.

Once you have chosen your design, make a preliminary sketch. Begin with a simple motif like the fish illustrated on page 21. The design can be drawn or traced with a soft pencil on to the material, either before or after it is pinned to the frame. Find the way that suits *you* best. When drawing a design on to silk, use a very soft blunt pencil, as a sharp point could damage the silk.

Batik frames can be scaled up to fit the material, but the size of the design will depend on the size of your frame. Whether you decide to apply the design before or after pinning the fabric to the frame, you may find it necessary to re-draw the pencil marks as your batik progresses. These pencil lines will disappear in the final boiling out or ironing off processes. If you are using silk, the frame should be bound with strips of material and covered with plastic. Always wipe any dye off the plastic between uses.

If you are using a frame, stretch the fabric as taut as possible over the edges, using dress-makers' pins or masking tape for silk and drawing pins for heavier fabrics. It is very important to ensure that the fabric is smooth and evenly stretched to enable the wax to be applied accurately and to prevent the cloth from sticking to the working surface. Start attaching the pins in the middle on opposite sides of the frame and continue outwards to the sides, stretching as you go.

If you are not using a frame, the working surface has to be smooth and flat. If you are painting dye on to the fabric lay the material on several sheets of newspaper; if you are applying wax lay the material on a sheet of greaseproof paper.

Transferring the design

You can transfer your design on to the fabric in a variety of ways. Place some tracing paper over the preliminary sketch and trace the design with indian ink. If you are using a thin, transparent fabric, simply place the design on to a light-coloured surface; place the material over it – the design can be clearly seen through the fabric. Trace on to the surface of the cloth with a soft pencil.

If your material is thick, or closely woven, tape or pin the traced design under the fabric and place both on a sheet of glass, smaller than the frame. If you light this sheet up from underneath, the design can be seen clearly through the material. Trace the design as described above.

Templates can be made or alternatively, just sketch the design directly on to the fabric.

Waxing

Make sure your working surface is covered with newspaper before starting to wax. If you are using a proper wax pot it will control the temperature of the wax thermostatically. If you melt the wax in the double saucepan, keep the melted wax hot by keeping the water boiling softly while the work of application is in progress.

The wax should be gently heated until it flows like water and will impregnate the fabric fibres. Ensure that the wax is ready for use by testing a small amount on the edge of some cotton fabric. When it appears transparent, it has penetrated the cloth, but if the wax appears opaque it is not quite hot enough.

If you are using silk, the same waxing method as for cotton applies, but you will find that the wax penetrates the silk very easily, making it harder to control, so do not overload your brush. Take care with the tjanting for the same reason. Also, paraffin wax cracks easily on silk, so bear this in mind.

First wax those areas that are to remain white, using either a brush or tjanting. Use the tjanting for fine lines and small areas. Hold a pad of newspaper under the tjanting or brush when moving from the wax pot to the fabric to ensure that the wax does not drip on to your work.

When covering large areas with wax use a large brush and force the wax into the fabric. Keep dipping the brush into the hot wax, as the wax cools very quickly.

When using the tjanting keep it in the hot wax until needed and then tip most of the wax

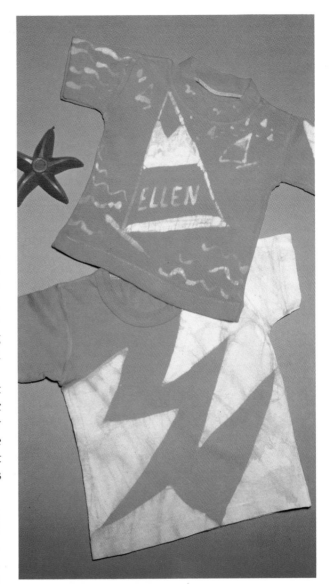

T-shirt designs by Heather Griffin
By purchasing ready made white cotton T-shirts and applying just one dye, lovely original designs can easily be created.
Above: size 3-6 months. Newspaper covered with greaseproof paper is placed inside the T-shirt, to separate front and back. The sailboards and baby's name are drawn or traced on to the front in pencil, and waxed using a tjanting and a small brush. The garment is then turned over and the process repeated with a slightly different sailboard design on the back. The paper is removed and the T-shirt dipped in scarlet dye. When dry, the wax is boiled out.
Below: size 18 months. The zig-zag design is drawn on to the front in pencil and the shirt is then placed on a sheet of greaseproof paper. Hot wax is applied by brush to the area that is to remain white and forced through the double thickness of the material. The T-shirt is then dipped in scarlet dye. When dry the wax is boiled out.

15

out of the reservoir, leaving only enough to run freely from the spout. This technique is not easy and it requires practice and patience to perfect.

Check the back of the batik from time to time to ensure that all areas have been penetrated by the wax. If not, turn the fabric over and rewax the back of the material where necessary. Mistakes made at this stage are not easy to correct, for once the wax is applied to the fabric it is difficult to remove, although not impossible.

Waxing double thicknesses of cotton

It is possible to wax through double thicknesses of cotton and silk, when you wish to have an identical design on both sides. On an item or garment that is already made up this is obviously a useful way to work.

Ensure that the double material is pulled taut on the frame. When waxing, force the hot wax through both thicknesses of cloth. Keep checking the underside of the material and re-wax if necessary.

Proceed with the dyeing and waxing as usual, taking care not to separate the two pieces of fabric until you reach the final stage of removing the wax.

If you do not wish to carry a design through to the back of a ready-made item, it is possible to separate the back and front by inserting greaseproof paper between the thicknesses.

Mistakes in waxing

To remove an unwanted area of wax, scrape as much wax as possible from both sides of the fabric with a knife. Then rub the area with a metal teaspoon that has been immersed in boiling water. Repeat the treatment until all the wax has been removed. The fabric must be completely free of wax before the dye can penetrate.

If, during the waxing process, the temperature of the wax has cooled giving an area of opaque wax, remove this carefully with a knife and re-wax.

Dyeing

We use the same dyes for silk as for cotton but the biggest difference is in the depth and tone of the colour. On silk the same solution of dye is sometimes several shades lighter than on cotton. Therefore, if you want to obtain deeper shades, you have to mix a stronger dye solution. There are special dyes available for use on silk only.

Now you are ready for the first dye. Mix your chosen colour with the fixatives as instructed by the manufacturer and pour the dye into a dye bath, first checking that it has been thoroughly mixed. Make sure the dye bath is large enough to allow the batik to be submerged easily and moved about.

Remember, the dyeing process always proceeds stage by stage from the lightest to the darkest colour.

Remove the cloth from the frame and, wearing rubber gloves and an apron, immerse the batik in the dye, keeping the fabric as flat as possible otherwise the wax will crack at this early stage.

If you deliberately want to introduce the fine lines that give batik its characteristic look at this early stage, just gently crumple the material before submerging it in the dye. This will 'crack' the wax, and the dye can penetrate the cloth. During the dyeing processes the dyes will automatically penetrate any cracks that may appear.

Ensure that the dye has penetrated the unwaxed fabric and remove it from the dye bath. Bear in mind that colours show up stronger on wet fabric. To get more of an idea of the shade, hold the batik up to a light or a window. If the colour is not strong enough, make a stronger mixture and submerge the

Detail from random-patterned waistcoat by Margaret Hone
Different colours are mixed and randomly applied to white cotton, which is then waxed. A final dipping in black dye creates the lovely design shown opposite. For detailed instructions see page 37.

fabric in the dye once more. Never fold a wet batik, as the dye will collect in the folds.

Do not wring the cloth, but using plastic pegs hang the batik up to dry by an outside edge, ensuring that the cloth is pulled taut on the line. Leave the dye bath underneath to catch the dripping dye. Never leave your batik hanging outside when it is raining, as spots of rain will weaken the dye.

A hand held hair dryer, or fan heater, can sometimes be useful for drying quickly indoors, but take care not to place your batik too near the heat, or this will melt the wax!

When the fabric is completely dry, return it to the frame and repeat the process with more wax and the second colour. Never attempt to wax damp fabric, as the wax will not be effective.

Continue repeating this process until you have used all the dyes you require for your batik. Areas that are waxed may need re-waxing if they are put through several dye baths. If you are using thicker fabrics, coat the back of the material as well, to make sure the areas are completely covered.

When you have reached the last and darkest colour of your scheme, and the cloth has been dry for at least two hours (but much longer if possible, preferably overnight), you are ready to remove the wax.

During the waxing and dyeing process, the dye can also be applied directly on to the fabric with a brush.

Painting on dye

After the first stage of 'wax-blocking', colours can be applied to the fabric using a brush and without dipping the batik into a dye. There are several benefits in using this technique:—
1. It is an economical process, as only a small amount of dye is needed.
2. It is a much quicker method for adding small areas of colour.
3. Minute details can be painted with a very fine brush, but only where areas are already enclosed by wax.
4. If a confined area of cracking is required, dye can be painted straight on to the already cracked wax, taking care to ensure that the dye thoroughly penetrates the cracks and is prevented from running into surrounding areas.
5. Gradation of colour can be achieved by the use of water in some areas to weaken the dye. To obtain gradation in colour, angle the fabric slightly, allowing the colour to run to the edge of the area you are painting.

Make sure that the frame is completely flat and that there is plenty of newspaper underneath it to absorb any dye that soaks through the cloth. If working on a very large piece of material which is too big for your frame, lay the fabric as flat as possible on the floor on several sheets of newspaper. Always cover the areas not to be dyed with newspaper to protect them from any dye that might drip from the brush. Take special care with this if working on a large piece of cloth.

Have ready jam jars containing the dyes to be used, a selection of brushes and a large jar of cold water. When painting the dye on to your fabric ensure that it thoroughly penetrates the cloth by forcing it into the material with the brush.

It is important always to have a jar of cold water handy. Water is used for many things including cleaning brushes between colour applications, washing out errors if the dye runs the wrong way and also for diluting the colour if necessary.

Absorbent paper tissues should be on hand for blotting up surplus dye and water.

Always, after use, thoroughly clean the dye bath, gloves and other materials. It is easier to clean everything properly at this stage, rather than having to remove unwanted dye from your next project. Remember also to wipe the clothes line and wash the plastic pegs.

Bleaching

Careful use of bleach on cotton can produce unusual effects. *Never* use bleach on silk, and always wear rubber gloves when using it.

A solution of one part bleach to two parts water can be used for washing out an unwanted shade of dye; or by cracking the wax on your batik (gently crumpling the fabric when the wax is cold) and laying it for a short while in the same solution of bleach and water, it is possible to obtain a reverse cracking effect, i.e. light cracking on dark colours.

Only immerse the areas of fabric you want bleached and keep other areas away from the solution and rinsing water. Rinse the cloth thoroughly with cold water as soon as the desired effect has been reached.

Removing wax

The two main ways of removing wax are by boiling and ironing. With cotton and heavier fabrics we prefer to boil out the wax, but we *never* use this method on silk, (see below).

Boiling out: for this stage you will need a large saucepan or metal bucket and wooden tongs. First flake as much wax as possible off the fabric on to newspaper. Then immerse the cloth in a large pan of very hot water, bring to the boil and boil for three minutes to remove the wax and set the dye. Use plenty of water for boiling out and make sure the material is fully covered. This is more difficult with large pieces of material, but equally important. Use wooden tongs to push the fabric down in the water taking care to avoid the hot, waxy water splashing on to your hands.

Using the tongs, plunge your batik into a plastic bucket of cold water. The cold water will solidify a great deal of the wax, which can be removed from the water by using a metal strainer. This wax is then ready for recycling, together with the loose wax collected on the newspaper. Again, the loose wax can be shaken off your batik on to newspaper and the fabric rinsed again in fresh cold water.

Repeat the process with clean hot water, boiling for only one minute this time. Two boilings are usually sufficient but a large area of heavily waxed cloth may require more. If too much loose wax remains on your material after it has been rinsed in the second bucket of cold water you will know that you have to repeat the boiling process.

Finally, boil your batik in water to which a good quality liquid detergent has been added to ensure complete removal of any remaining wax. (Poor quality detergents are less efficient and small particles of wax may remain in the cloth if they are used). After a last cold water rinse the fabric can be washed and dried like any normal material.

Never attempt to recycle any wax that has been mixed with detergent and never under any circumstances put the hot or cold waxy water down the sink as it could block the drain!

Ironing off: flake off wax as before and place your batik between layers of absorbent paper and on several sheets of newspaper. Iron, using the correct setting recommended for the fabric, constantly changing the paper as it becomes saturated with wax. Old newspapers can be used, but there is a danger of newsprint being deposited on your fabric, so it is best to sandwich the batik between sheets of plain white absorbent paper. Decorators' lining paper can be used or blotting paper.

Be sure to wipe off any surplus dye left on the surface of the wax before you iron off, otherwise unwanted colour may be forced into your material. If, when ironing the finished batik, you should discover small wax marks, these can be removed by applying cleaning solvent or concentrated liquid detergent and boiling water.

Removal of wax on silk

Because of the delicacy of silk, the wax must never be removed by the boiling method. The wax can either be partially flaked off and 'ironed off' as for cotton. This method can be used for pictures, wallhangings, etc; or the wax can be partially flaked off and the silk dry-cleaned. If you attempt to apply batik to a ready-made garment in silk, it will be extremely difficult to ensure complete removal of the wax, as it may be trapped in seams and double thicknesses of fabric. We therefore recommend dry-cleaning.

Alternatively, with garments that require frequent washing, we prefer the following method.

19

NORTHEAST TEXAS COMMUNITY COLLEGE LEARNING RESOURCE CENTER MT PLEASANT TEXAS 75455 WITHDRAWN

Flake off as much wax as possible on to newspaper. Place the batik in a bucket. Pour boiling water over the silk and leave it to stand for three minutes. You will find wooden tongs are useful for moving the material around in the water. Using the tongs transfer the silk from the hot water to a bucket of cold water. Remove silk from the cold water shaking off any loose wax. Empty the hot water into the cold to solidify the wax and remove this for recycling.

Repeat the process with fresh water allowing the silk to stand in the boiling water for about one minute. Finally, add liquid detergent to the boiling water and proceed as before but do not attempt to recycle any wax you may have in the detergent water.

Finish off by washing and ironing normally, using a fabric conditioner in the last rinse.

Recycling the wax

Collect together all the wax that has been removed from your batik, place it in a saucepan of clean water and boil for about twenty minutes. When cold, the wax will solidify on top of the water and can easily be removed from the saucepan. Scrape the sediment from the underside of the wax. This clean wax is now ready for re-use.

Useful points to remember

After dyeing, never leave your batik hanging outside when it is raining, as spots of rain will weaken the dye

Never fold a wet batik as the dye will collect in the folds of the material

A hand-held hair dryer, or a fan heater, can sometimes be useful for drying fabric quickly indoors, but take care not to place your batik too near the heat or this will melt the wax.

Never attempt to wax material that is damp as the wax will not be effective

When boiling wax out of the material, use plenty of water and make sure the material is fully covered. This is more difficult with large pieces of fabric, but equally important. Use wooden tongs to push the material down in to the water, taking care to avoid the hot, waxy water splashing on to your hands.

Use a good quality liquid detergent to ensure complete removal of small particles of wax from the cloth. Poor quality detergents are less efficient.

When ironing off wax, decorators' lining paper can be used as well as white absorbent paper.

If, when ironing the finished batik, you should discover small wax marks, these can be removed by cleaning solvent, or by concentrated liquid detergent and boiling water.

Projects

The projects in this section range from simple bows and scarves to more complicated batik designs which are achieved by using a variety of dyes. Because of the nature of batik, it is impossible to foresee what exactly will happen during the waxing and dyeing processes as wax cracks and colours mix and blend. Through experimenting you will discover how this can be used to the best advantage.

Always allow twenty four hours for your batik to dry between dyeing and waxing.

Simple fish motif to show technique

This simply illustrates how to apply the techniques shown on the previous pages.

The outlines of this fish motif lend themselves particularly well to batik, see page 25 for finished illustration. The finished batik can be framed, or made into a wallhanging. Here we give instructions for a wallhanging. Details on framing can be found on page 46.

Materials

White cotton poplin 46 × 61 cm (18 × 24 in), noting that 5 cm (2 in) is allowed all round for pinning the fabric to the frame, giving a finished size of 35.5 × 51 cm (14 × 20 in).
Yellow, red, blue dyes
Wax
Two lengths of wooden dowelling, 38 cm (15in) long
Length of cord, as required.

Method

First draw a sketch plan of the colour sequence you require. We have used yellow, red and blue, but you could choose your own colour sequence.

sketch plan to show colour sequence

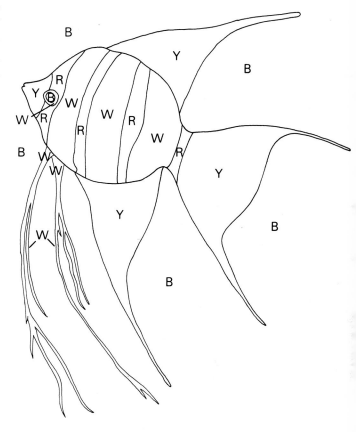

Colour key

W = white
Y = yellow
R = red, making orange
B = blue, making brown

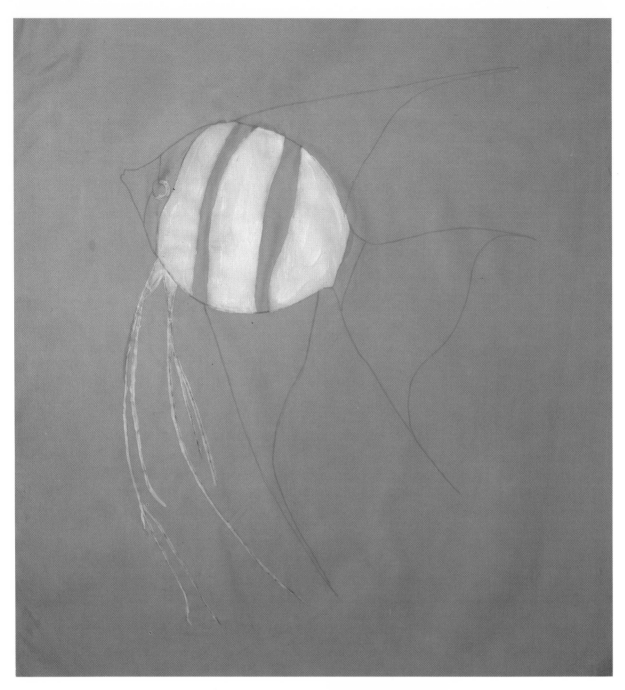

Draw the outline of the fish on to the fabric, then wax the areas to be kept white and dip in the yellow dye. Hang the batik up to dry.

When dry, wax areas to be kept yellow and dip in red dye to give orange. Hang the batik up to dry.

When dry, wax areas to be kept orange and lightly crack the design by gently crumpling the fabric, before dipping the batik into the final blue dye. This gives a brown background with blue cracks on the white areas, green on the yellow and brown on the orange. Leave to dry overnight and remove the wax by the boiling method.

After the wax has been removed and the batik has been allowed to dry, the colours appear much lighter. Now you can make your wallhanging.

Neaten your completed batik by trimming off approximately 2.5 cm (1 in) all round the edges.

Now hem the long side edges and make open-ended hems, at top and bottom edges. Allow enough space to insert the wooden dowelling. Insert wooden dowelling into top and bottom hems and attach a length of cord to the top edge.

Bow designs by Margaret Hone

Bows

These bows are all designed by Margaret Hone. They can be made quite effectively from small scraps of material left over from a larger garment, and can, of course, also be made deliberately to suit any colour scheme. The one colour on white effect is an example of batik in its simplest form but it is still effective as a basic colour scheme.

The bows illustrated are just simple bows but you can, of course, make them double or even triple, as long as you make each bow slightly larger than the one in front of it. The illustrations in this book are for a single bow and are really easy for even the inexperienced needle-woman to follow.

The instructions below are for the pink and white bow shown at the top of this page. Use the techniques in this book to create your own original batik designs.

Materials

White cotton poplin 40 × 15 cm (15 ¾ × 6 in) for the bow
White cotton poplin 7.5 × 5 cm (3 × 2in) for the knot
Dyes and wax, as required

26

Method

Stretch the material on the frame. Using a brush and wax, apply an abstract design to the fabric. Dye the fabric, deliberately introducing cracks in the wax by gently crumpling the material while it is immersed in the dye, so allowing the dye to penetrate the cloth to achieve a veined pattern. Leave to dry and remove the wax by the boiling method.

To complete

Hem long sides of larger piece of fabric. With wrong sides together, fold bow at marked fold lines, overlapping the short ends in the centre.

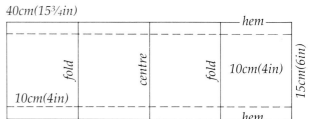

Stitch along centre line through all thicknesses of material.

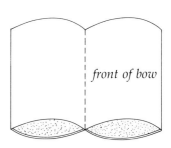

Make gathers by sewing two lines of large stitches on each side of the centre line and about 6 mm (¼in) away from it. Pull the thread and gather the stitches up to about 5 cm (2 in) in length.

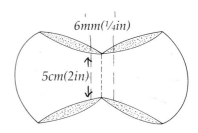

Fold long ends of smaller piece of fabric to inside and press to form knot.

folding the knot

Use scraps of cotton left over from a larger garment to make a matching bow. Here areas of wax, and yellow, red and blue dyes, are applied to a remnant of white cotton poplin, creating a lovely mixture of colours and patterns.

Wrap knot round the middle of the bow, pulling it tight to gather up the centre, then secure it at the back.

back of bow

An abstract design is waxed on to dupion silk before the fabric is dipped in to an orange dye. If you want to deliberately introduce cracks in to the design, gently crumple the silk while it is immersed in the dye.

These bows can be sewn on to hair combs, hair grips, head-bands or pony tail ties, or used to decorate clothing. You can, of course, quite easily make the bow larger or smaller by adjusting the measurements given.

Silk scarves

A silk scarf complemented with an original design is an ideal gift or accessory. These scarves were purchased already made up and the fine silk gives a delicate effect, even with quite strong dyes. It is not possible to make very strong contrasts in colours on this material, although heavier silks such as crepe de Chine, silk satin and silk twill react better to stronger dyes.

The scarves opposite demonstrate that batik on fine lightweight silk achieves rather lovely effects. They are all made by the same method. This method is explained below, taking the scarf in the top left of the picture as the example. Use the techniques described earlier in this book to create designs like the ones shown opposite.

Materials

1 purchased white Habotai silk square, 90 × 90cm (35 ½ × 35 ½ in).
Blue, red, brown dyes
Microcrystalline wax

Method

Very simple techniques are used to create this lovely scarf. Although three dyes are used, there is only one colour dipping. Small amounts of wax are used making possible the addition of several other colours by painting on. The white silk scarf is laid on greaseproof paper and using a 2.5 cm (1 in) wide brush an abstract 'starfish' design is painted on to the fabric with the melted wax.

When the wax has cooled, the scarf is laid flat in strong blue dye for a few minutes. It is then removed and laid out flat on clean, dry newspaper.

It is better to dry fine silk scarves in this way, rather than hanging them up, as there is less likelihood of damage. The newspaper absorbs the dye quickly, resulting in a lighter colour. Large sheets of plastic can be used for the same purpose, but the dye will not be absorbed and therefore a deeper colour may be obtained.

When the blue dye has dried, the scarf is laid out on greaseproof paper again for rewaxing. Some small dribbles of wax are allowed to run on to the blue silk, enclosing areas of the fabric. This will act as a barrier to the dyes used in the final process.

When the wax is cold, the scarf is laid on newspaper. Small amounts of red and brown dyes are mixed in separate jars and painted on to the scarf, filling in the spaces enclosed by wax only. Some blue areas are left unpainted. The red dye turns mauve as it mixes with the background blue, and the brown dye is used as a contrast against the lighter colours.

The scarf is left to dry overnight and the wax removed, (see page 19).

Silk scarf designs by Margaret Hone
Lovely delicate effects can be achieved by applying wax and dyes to silk. The colours and patterns on the scarves shown opposite are all created using the techniques illustrated in this book.

Multicoloured silk top

Lightweight silk and soft colours are used to enhance this pretty top. There is no need to attach silk to a frame when the design is a simple one especially when the silk used is fairly delicate.

Materials

Purchased pattern
White Habotai silk as required
Light blue, yellow, red, brown, orange dyes
Microcrystalline wax

Method

The pattern pieces are first cut to size before being spread out separately on clean dry newspaper. Two jars of light blue and yellow dye, and a jar of clean water are prepared. Small areas of the colours are applied to the silk using a 2.5 cm (1 in) wide brush. The water is used to keep the two colours apart where they threaten to merge (paint the water on to the fabric over the areas where blending may occur); it is also used to clean the brush between colour applications.

The silk is then spread out on newspaper to dry. When it is completely dry it is transferred to greaseproof paper and an abstract leafy design is waxed on to the fabric using a small brush.

After the wax has cooled, the pieces of silk are transferred once more on to clean dry newspaper and small amounts of red, brown and orange dyes are mixed in separate jars. These colours are applied in a random way to the unwaxed areas with lovely effects where the colours overlap.

The silk is left to dry overnight and the wax removed in the usual way, (see page 19). Make up the pattern as directed.

Random patterned top

Several shades of red and blue blend and mix to create a lovely effect on this design. A heavier weight of Habotai silk is used; consequently the colours are stronger and more vibrant and the fabric is easier to handle.

Silk top by Margaret Hone

Random patterned top by Margaret Hone

Materials

Purchased pattern
Habotai silk as required, medium weight
Red, blue, turquoise, brilliant red and black dyes
Microcrystalline wax

Method

The pattern pieces are cut out and then spread out on clean dry newspaper. Areas of pale red and pale blue dye are randomly painted on to the fabric using a 2.5 cm (1 in) wide brush. Water is painted liberally on to the areas of silk to be left undyed to prevent the colours running into one another.

The silk pieces are transferred on to more newspaper to dry out. When dry, they are transferred to greaseproof paper and an abstract leafy design is waxed on to the fabric. The silk is then once more returned to clean dry newspaper.

Turquoise, brilliant red and black dyes are mixed separately and a jar of clean water is prepared to clean the brush between colour applications. The three colours are added to the silk in a random way, but with some thought given to the balance of the colours throughout. The silk is dried out overnight and the wax then removed, (see page 19).

Make up the pattern as directed.

Simple summer top

A medium weight crepe de Chine is simply waxed and dyed using 2 shades of turquoise and very little red. This type of silk is lovely to work with as it is not too light.

Materials

Purchased pattern
White crepe de Chine, as required
Turquoise, red dyes
Microcrystalline wax

Method

The pattern pieces are cut out. The silk is then dipped into a pale turquoise dye and hung out to dry.

When dry, the silk is spread out on greaseproof paper and random lines are waxed from top to bottom using a 2.5 cm (1 in) brush. The garment pieces are then dipped into a stronger version of the same turquoise dye and again hung out to dry.

When dry, the silk is again returned to the greaseproof paper and further lines are waxed on to the fabric.

The unwaxed area is now quite small and the silk is finally dipped in a red dye, turning these unwaxed areas mauve. A few cracks are introduced to the wax at this stage so the red dye penetrates through, producing a lovely veined effect. The silk is dried overnight and the wax is removed the next day, (see page 19).

When the silk is dry, make up the pattern as directed.

Simple summer top by Margaret Hone

Silk summer top

Three dyes are used on this simple silk top to create a batik landscape in greens and blues.

Materials

Purchased pattern
White silk crepe de Chine, as required
Turquoise, yellow, royal blue dyes
Paraffin wax

Method

The silk is cut into two pieces; these are placed together and pinned with dressmakers' pins to a bound frame; then the outline of the back of the garment is drawn lightly on to the top of the silk in pencil, using the pattern as a guide.

The chosen design is pencilled on to the silk, within the pattern area, and then the wax is applied through the double thickness of silk to the areas to remain white – tree trunks, clouds, fences and cottages. It is advisable to check the back of the silk pieces before continuing, to make sure the wax has penetrated the two thicknesses. If not, turn the frame over and retouch areas that need waxing.

When the wax is cold, the silk is unpinned from the frame, keeping the two pieces together by pinning the edges – in parts they are already firmly held together by the wax, the pins are an added precaution to prevent the two pieces separating during the dyeing processes. The top is dipped in turquoise dye.

When dry, the silk is transferred to the frame and tree shapes, foliage and hedgerows waxed over the turquoise. Yellow dye is painted on to make green.

When dry, the whole area of silk is covered with wax. When it is cold, the sky and trees are deliberately cracked by crumpling the silk

Silk summer top and cropped cotton top
by Heather Griffin
A simple landscape theme gives life and colour to two white summer tops. Whether you purchase a pattern (left), or buy a garment (right), beautiful batik designs can be applied by following a few basic rules.
The picture below right shows a detail of the cropped cotton top above.

and then it is dipped into a strong royal blue dye.

The wax is removed by the hot water method, (see page 19). When the silk is dry, it is ready to be made up according to the pattern instructions. Carefully match the batik design when making up the garment.

Cropped cotton top

A purchased white cotton top is enhanced by a lovely pale summery batik landscape which is drawn on to the fabric freehand, using sketches as reference.

Materials

Purchased white cotton top
Pale blue, bright yellow, turquoise, red, brown, dark blue dyes
Paraffin wax

Method

The design on the back of the top is the same as the design on the front (only in reverse). So the wax is worked through the double thickness of cloth.

Before starting, a decision is made about which areas are to remain white. In this design it is the cottages (apart from the roofs), fences and the flowers in the foreground of the landscape. These areas are waxed, using a tjanting and several brushes, depending on the size of the area.

Pale blue dye is painted on to the top to represent 'sky' and yellow dye painted on to represent 'fields'. Where the two colours meet water is brushed on to blend and weaken the dye; this is then blotted with kitchen paper.

The top 'sky' section and some of the yellow 'fields' are waxed leaving areas free. These will appear as hedges, trees and grass.

The top is then dipped in turquoise blue and the 'sky' deliberately cracked by gently crumpling the fabric.

The green that results from the dipping is then kept by waxing. The cottage roofs are waxed round and when enclosed, some red and brown dyes are painted on. When dry these are waxed.

Finally, the waxed top is lightly cracked by crumpling, and then dipped in dark blue dye. Care is taken to keep the 'sky' section out of the dye bath, so that no dark cracking occurs on this area.

When dry the wax is boiled out.

Sleeveless top

The same landscape theme is used on this sleeveless top. Again the design is based on sketches and transferred to the fabric freehand.

Materials

Purchased pattern
White cotton poplin as required
Yellow, red, blue, turquoise dyes
Paraffin wax

Method

The material is cut in half and the two pieces placed together and pinned to a frame. The paper pattern and design outlines are drawn on to the material. When waxing and dyeing, carry the design out beyond the pattern lines.

Sleeveless top by Heather Griffin
The enlarged detail opposite shows the reverse side of the garment and it illustrates clearly how wax is applied to this garment to retain white areas of cotton. Cottage walls, fences and trees are waxed on to the fabric before the initial dyes are applied.

Using a tjanting and a brush, wax is applied to the areas to remain white – sky, fences, road, tree trunks and cottage walls.

Yellow dye is painted on to the material, through both thicknesses, then red dye is applied alongside the 'road'. Where the two colours merge they become orange.

The yellow areas are waxed, leaving the tree areas free. Blue dye is painted on to give a lovely leafy yellowy green. These areas are then waxed and red is painted on to the cottage roofs. When dry the roofs are waxed.

The wax covering the sky is deliberately cracked, by folding the material into horizontal lines and the whole top is removed from the frame and dipped in turquoise dye. The wax will hold the two pieces of material together, but a few dressmakers' pins attached around the edges of the fabric will ensure they will not come apart during the dyeing process.

The wax is boiled out once the material is dry. Once all the wax is removed and the material is dry, make up the pattern as directed.

Summer waistcoat

White, turquoise and yellow blend to create a light summery feel. The waxed areas are heavily cracked to heighten this effect and to break up the overall white look, without losing the feeling of freshness.

Materials

Purchased waistcoat pattern
White cotton poplin, as required
Yellow, orange, turquoise dyes
Microcrystalline wax

Method

The pattern pieces are cut out of the cotton material and the lining put to one side. The remaining pieces of cotton are laid separately on to newspaper and areas of yellow and orange dye are painted directly on to the fabric. When dry the pieces of cotton are transferred on to greaseproof paper and using a 5 cm (2 in) wide paint brush, broad semicircular lines are waxed randomly on to the material.

When the wax has cooled, the material is dipped in strong turquoise dye, and the wax is deliberately cracked so that veins of turquoise will appear on the fabric.
The boiling out process is left until the next day and the waistcoat is made up according to the pattern instructions.

Random patterned waistcoat

Beautiful random designs are easily applied using batik. Lovely colours have been used to brighten up this simple waistcoat.

Materials

Purchased waistcoat pattern
White cotton poplin, as required
Red, yellow, blue, black dyes
Microcrystalline wax

Method

Three jars of dye are made up; red, yellow and blue. Two more colours are obtained by combining red and blue to give mauve, and blue and yellow to give green. The pieces of cotton are cut out and the lining pieces are set to one side, as they are to remain white in contrast to the bright colours that are to be applied to the outside of the garment.
The remaining pieces of cotton are laid separately on to sheets of newspaper and random areas of the five colours are painted on, overlapping in some areas and leaving white areas in others.
When dry the pieces of material are placed on greaseproof paper, and an abstract design waxed over the colours. When the wax is cold,

Waistcoat designs by Margaret Hone
Simple waistcoat patterns take on a fresh original look when batik is applied to white cotton. Dyes are painted on to the cut-out pattern pieces, then wax is applied before the final dipping in a dye bath. After the boiling out process, the fabric is allowed to dry and the garments are made up as directed.

it is lightly cracked, by crumpling the batik gently, and the material is laid in a dye bath containing black dye for five minutes.

The boiling out process is left until the next day.

Once the material is completely dry, the waist-coat is made up according to the pattern instructions. The final result is a brightly coloured garment with a contrasting white lining.

Summer shirts for men

The two shirts shown here illustrate how batik can transform ordinary white cotton shirts into striking designs, using bold, vibrant colours. Both 'painting-on' and the dipping of dyes are used to create the colours and patterns, which are planned from sketches and photographs.

Materials

2 purchased white cotton shirts
Paraffin wax
'Jungle' shirt: yellow, red, turquoise, brilliant blue, royal blue dyes
'Sailboard' shirt: yellow, turquoise, royal blue, brilliant red dyes

Method

The designs are drawn, or traced, on to the shirts. During the waxing and dyeing process, the fronts and backs of the shirts are worked separately. Each section is spread out flat – on greaseproof paper while waxing, and on newspaper while painting. Greaseproof paper is inserted into the sleeves.

'Jungle' shirt: hot wax is applied over the areas to remain white, on the single thickness of fabric, using a tjanting and brushes.

The shirt is then spread out on newspaper and yellow and red dyes randomly painted on, allowing the colours to merge in places. Water and a weak solution of turquoise dye are brushed on between the red and yellow areas. Care is taken to apply the colours to the back of the sleeves. Areas of red and yellow are retained by waxing and leaf shapes are waxed on to the fabric.

When dry, more leaf and tree shapes are waxed on to the fabric and the palm tree trunks cracked by pinching the waxed cloth. The shirt is then dipped in brilliant blue dye.

When dry, more shapes are waxed on and the final dipping is in royal blue dye.

When dry, the wax is boiled out.

Shirt designs by Heather Griffin
A holiday wardrobe can be livened up by applying dyes and wax to ready-made white cotton shirts. Here, the jungle and a seascape offer inspiration for two colourful designs.

'**Sailboard' shirt**: The same method of painting, waxing and dyeing is used. The sailboard outlines are waxed, then green (turquoise and yellow) is painted on some sails. The green areas are waxed and the shirt is dipped in turquoise dye.

The turquoise is then waxed in some areas and the shirt dipped in blue dye.

The shirt is then waxed through the double thickness of fabric to create the impression of waves, before finally dipping it in brilliant red dye.

When dry the wax is boiled out.

Landscape shirt

The batik design on this shirt was freely adapted from sketches and photographs, to give the impression of a landscape. The blue on the collar represents sky and a stream meanders round the hips, separating green fields from wooded slopes. When creating a design like this, always expect the unexpected! The original design constantly changes throughout the waxing and dyeing processes as colours mix and blend. Follow the guidelines below to create your own unique design.

Materials

Ready-made purchased long-sleeved baggy shirt in white cotton
Turquoise, yellow, brilliant blue, royal blue, brilliant red dyes
Paraffin wax

Method

The buttons are removed and pencil guidelines indicating the position of cottages, fields and the skyline are drawn on to the shirt.

The shirt is laid out flat on a sheet of greaseproof paper in preparation for waxing. It is waxed from the front, through the double thickness, giving the same design in reverse on the back. First all the areas to remain white are waxed i.e clouds, cottage walls, fences and flowers.

As the next stage is painting the dye on to the fabric, the shirt is transferred on to newspaper (or absorbent paper) and the colours applied through the double thickness. Yellow and a weak mix of brilliant blue are made up and applied to the material using large brushes. The yellow is painted on to represent fields and the blue to represent sky (on the collar) and the stream. With a small brush a weak mix of brilliant red is painted on to the cottage roofs.

Check the back of the shirt to make sure the colours have penetrated the double thickness and retouch any areas that need colour. Colours may spread or blend on the fabric. Don't worry, these can be adapted as part of the landscape as the dyeing process continues!

When dry, the shirt is once more transferred on to a sheet of greaseproof paper. Wax is applied over the yellow fields, the blue sky and stream, and the cottage roofs. Areas where the blue and yellow dyes have merged to create green, are waxed into tree shapes.

The shirt is then dipped in the turquoise dye. When dry, wax is again applied over certain areas of the turquoise. This creates turquoise trees, a wooded skyline, a turquoise cottage roof and flowers and grasses.

The shirt is then dipped in yellow dye. The unwaxed turquoise areas blend with the yellow dye to give green.

When dry, wax is applied to the fields, and some trees and hedges. The final dipping is in royal blue dye.

The wax is boiled out. Several boilings are needed and care must be taken to squeeze out the collar and cuffs so that hard lumps of wax do not collect in the double thicknesses and seams when the shirt is plunged into cold water. Rinse the shirt in cold water each time after boiling.

Shirt design by Heather Griffin
This landscape design is gradually built up by freehand waxing and dyeing. Areas are waxed on to the plain white fabric to represent clouds, cottages, fences and flowers, and yellows and blues merge and mix to give green fields, hedges and trees. The picture on the right shows a detail of the finished design.

Summer coat

Vibrant colours transform a simple shirt into a lovely summer coat. A purchased shirt pattern is used, but the garment is cut longer than the original design by extending the pattern guidelines and extra large pockets are added as a special feature. The design is simplified by omitting buttons and buttonholes, and no frame is used when waxing and dyeing because of the large size of the pieces of fabric.

Materials

Purchased pattern
White cotton poplin as required
Pale blue, red, yellow dyes
Microcrystalline wax

Method

Large pieces of material are difficult to handle when wet, so the fabric is cut into two smaller pieces. The best way to do this is to lay the pattern pieces on to the material before deciding where to cut (remembering to remove the pattern pieces before commencing).

Lay the material on to clean dry newspaper and using a small brush paint on random areas of pale blue, pale red and yellow. When dry, transfer the pieces of material to large *flat* sheets of plastic. Large squares are waxed on to the dyed fabric using a 5cm (2in) brush. As the wax cools, the plastic will easily peel away. (A small amount of wax will be left on the plastic, so check the back of the fabric to see whether any re-waxing is required). The material is now dipped in a bright red/pink dye. Some red cracks will appear in the waxed areas at this stage.

After it has been hung out to dry, the material is again spread out on to plastic and re-waxed; lines are drawn in wax round the already waxed squared, making larger squares. In some areas the red cracks are re-waxed to prevent the next colour from penetrating them, but many are left.

The fabric is removed, as before, and placed in a fresh dye bath containing yellow dye. Again new cracks are made in the wax and now there are red and yellow cracks – and orange where the two colours have combined.

The wax is removed the next day, when the fabric is completely dry. After the final washing and ironing, cut out the pattern pieces and make up the garment as directed.

Coat design by Margaret Hone
A purchased shirt pattern is used to make a colourful summer coat. Red, yellow and blue dyes combine to create a lovely batik design.

Simple cotton coat

This simple design has no collar or buttons and it makes good use of lovely bold, contrasting colours. The material was found in a market and it was a real bargain! Useful material can often be found in markets, but be sure that any you buy for batik is pure cotton and not a synthetic fibre. The cotton used for this coat had to be washed thoroughly to soften it.

Materials

Purchased pattern
White cotton as required
Pale blue, yellow, red, orange, navy, black dyes
Microcrystalline wax

Simple cotton coat by Margaret Hone

Method

Before commencing, cut the material into manageable lengths, after the pattern pieces have been placed upon it for guidance. Dye these lengths in pale blue dye and hang them up to dry.

Transfer the material on to clean dry newspaper and paint on several lines of black dye. Allow to dry and then transfer the material to a frame and wax abstract leaf shapes over the surface using a small brush.

Lovely effects can be achieved at this stage by allowing the wax to drip haphazardly from the brush while tipping the frame up slightly. This encourages the wax to flow freely.

When the wax is dry, place plenty of newspapers under the frame and randomly paint on yellow, red, orange and navy dyes. Allow the dyes to overlap in some places to give different colours.

When the material is dry, remove the wax. After the final washing and ironing, cut out the pattern pieces and make up the garment as directed.

Summer coats

Pretty flower and leaf designs are applied in wax over random-dyed cotton poplin (above) and cotton lawn (below). These two coats illustrate the simple use of batik on large pieces of material, as there is only one waxing session on each garment.

Materials

2 purchased patterns
Microcrystalline wax
Random patterned coat (above) : white cotton poplin as required; red, blue, yellow dyes
Summer flower coat (below) : fine white cotton lawn as required; blue, yellow, green, tan dyes

Method for random patterned coat

Spread the material out on clean, dry newspaper and paint on random areas of red, blue and yellow, leaving some white spaces between the coloured areas. When the dyes are dry, transfer the material on to flat sheets of plastic and wax flower and leaf shapes over the whole surface.

Remove the material from the plastic sheets and transfer on to clean newspaper; apply red, yellow and blue dyes to the unwaxed areas in a random fashion. Leave the material to dry overnight and remove the wax the next day. After washing and ironing, cut out the pattern pieces and make up the garment as directed.

Method for summer flower coat

This coat is designed to retain much of the basic white of the cotton to give a fresh look. The material is cut into workable sections and a few random patches of pale red and blue are applied with a 2.5 cm (1 in) brush, after the material has been spread out on fresh dry newspaper. As only a small amount of the dye is used, the material is so fine it dries quickly on the absorbent paper. After transferring the material on to a sheet of plastic, a simple flower design is waxed freely over the surface.

Transfer the material on to clean, dry newspaper and paint yellow and tan dyes on to a few of the unwaxed areas that are now enclosed with wax. As very little colour is being added to the fabric each time, there is no need to dip the garment into the dye bath.

The wax is removed when the material is completely dry. After the final washing and ironing, cut out the pattern pieces and make up the garment as directed.

Random patterned coat by Margaret Hone

Summer flower coat by Margaret Hone

The Hollyford Track

This picture is based on a photograph of the Hollyford Track, a path which runs through the bush in New Zealand's South Island. It shows a much more involved use of colour and composition than the other projects, and is therefore not suitable for a beginner. However, it is an example of what can be achieved with patience and perseverance.

Materials

69 × 81 cm (27 × 32 in) white cotton, noting that 5 cm (2 in) is allowed all round for glueing the edges of the picture, giving a finished size of 63 × 76 cm (25 × 30 in)
Yellow, orange, red, brown, olive green, light and dark blue dyes
Paraffin wax

Method

The picture is worked on a frame. Pencil guidelines are made on the cotton, to indicate the main areas of light, and the shape of the path.

Wax is applied using a tjanting and a fine brush, to areas to be kept very light – tops of ferns, foliage and the light between trees.

Different strengths of yellow and orange dyes are painted on, using the photograph as reference, and water is brushed on to weaken the dye in the lightest areas.

Areas between the trees, branches and foliage are kept in wax, using the tjanting and a fine brush. Painting continues in this way, using red and a weak blue dye to create some greens and browns. Small sections are waxed, to retain varying colours and shapes.

The main shape of the distant light area is waxed, and the path, also green areas amongst the trees.

Red, green and brown dyes are freely painted on and waxed until the completed batik is covered in wax. This is then cracked by crushing and pinching the material to form patterns in the wax so creating the effect of foliage. It is then dipped in dark green dye.

When dry, the wax is boiled out so that the progression of colours can be checked. At this stage the design can be altered, or any shapes that are too light, changed. Areas that are to be retained are then rewaxed, some shapes altered and some new ones made. The line of the cracking can be followed with the wax, creating interesting branch shapes. The painting on of dyes and the waxing continue as before.

The darkest of the tree trunks are kept free of wax until the final dipping in dark blue which gives a dark brown. The waxed cotton is crumpled and folded to give some dark cracking, so adding to the impression of light and shade in the forest.

When dry, the wax is boiled out and the finished picture again allowed to dry.

To Complete

The following techniques for framing a batik may be used for both cotton and silk, but it may be advisable to cover a silk painting with glass for protection.

You may decide to make your own frame and in this event, a natural wooden frame is most effective and inexpensive. A professional picture framer could also mount and frame your batik, if you prefer.

A batik picture can be stretched over a piece of hardboard before it is framed. When calculating the size of the hardboard, allow at least 5 cm (2 in) *less* all round than the finished size of the fabric, so that the cloth can be overlapped all round and glued to the back of the board.

Paint the *smooth* side of the hardboard with white emulsion paint to give the best results. Allow to dry. Now stretch the batik firmly over the white painted side of the board, glue securely to the back with adhesive, and neaten the edges with masking tape.

Allow the mount to dry thoroughly before framing the picture.

The Hollyford Track by Heather Griffin

46

First published in the United States 1990
North Light Books
1507 Dana Avenue
Cincinnati, Ohio 45207

Copyright © 1989 Search Press Limited

Photographs by Search Press Studios

All rights reserved. No part of this book may be
reproduced in any form, by print, photoprint, microfilm,
microfiche, mechanical recording, photocopying,
translation, or any other means, known or as yet
unknown, or stored in an information retrieval system,
without written permission obtained beforehand from
Search Press Limited. Similarly, the items illustrated are
strictly copyright and may not be copied for commercial
purposes without the permission of Search Press Limited
to whom all enquiries in connection with this book or any
part of it should be addressed.

ISBN 0-89134-327-X

TT 852.5 .G75 1990
Griffin, Heather.
Introduction to batik

028050

00015413 2   DEMCO

Typeset by Scribe Design,
123 Watling Street,
Gillingham, Kent.
Printed in Spain by Artes Graphicas Elkar, S. Coop.
Autonomia, 71-48012-Bilbao – Spain.